D0299449

Repair the Broken Pieces

Repair the Broken Pieces

*A System to Awaken Positive Relations Between the Family
and Educational Provider Through Engagement Fusion*

Deborah M. Vereen, EdD

Copyright © 2017 by Deborah M. Vereen, EdD.

Library of Congress Control Number:		2017912870
ISBN:	Hardcover	978-1-5434-4545-9
	Softcover	978-1-5434-4544-2
	eBook	978-1-5434-4546-6

All rights reserved. No part of this book may be reproduced or transmitted in any form or by any means, electronic or mechanical, including photocopying, recording, or by any information storage and retrieval system, without permission in writing from the copyright owner.

Any people depicted in stock imagery provided by Thinkstock are models, and such images are being used for illustrative purposes only.
Certain stock imagery © Thinkstock.

Print information available on the last page.

Rev. date: 09/01/2017

To order additional copies of this book, contact:
Xlibris
1-888-795-4274
www.Xlibris.com
Orders@Xlibris.com
760361

"A must read for anyone who plays an instrumental role in the lives of children. Acknowledging the many facets in the lived experiences of children and parents, that impact learning, as well as the concrete, easy to follow recommendations to improve and increase parental engagement, provided in this book, will assist any individual advocating on behalf of children, in becoming the catalyst needed to repair the broken pieces of social and emotional instability and ensure academic success."

Jacqueline D. Wilson; Ph.D
CEO, Three Rivers Adoption Council
Adjunct Professor, University of Pittsburgh School of Social Work

"Reading Repair the Broken Pieces took me back to my first teaching job with the Los Angeles School District. It was 1969 and the Civil Rights Movement was beginning to hold sensitivity training sessions with the teachers to help us understand multicultural biases. I currently own and operate a gymnastics school in Pittsburgh and feel this book would be very beneficial for our entire staff. Although our coaches know gymnastics, few of them have had any professional training in educational psychology, child development or public relations. This book highlights the practical behaviors for coach-parent relations that will lead to successful outcomes for our gymnasts. I loved it and would recommend Repair the Broken Pieces as a must read for all club owners and their managers."

Mrs. Elaine Jewart.
President, Jewart's Gymnastics

"An excellent book underscoring research based techniques and best instructional strategies for family-school engagement that determines student success and their level of achievement."

Dr. Kenneth O. Barbour, Ph.D
Retired Principal - Riverview School District
Retired Principal - Hillcrest Christian Academy

"A visionary *must read* for every 21st **and** 22nd century educator. Dr. Vereen addresses the critical necessity of positive connections between educators and families they serve. Her book details concrete strategies for infusing this engagement process in a real-time manner for today and tomorrow!"

Agatha Campbell Leonard
Independent Contractor
Education Consultant, Special Education and Pupil Personnel Service

"Congratulations Dr. Vereen for providing a quick and easy read for all agencies who are privileged to interact with students and parents in various settings. Building trust and focusing on the positive are key components to student success. Dr. Cynthia Zurchin, Co-author, *The Whale Done! School*, Founder & Director, Cynthia's School of Dance & Music."

Dr. Cynthia Zurchin
Director, Cynthia's School of Dance & Music

"Sheer Brilliance! Dr. Vereen's "Repair the Broken Pieces" captures the importance of collaborative efforts. It combines all the necessary aspects of true community and working together while guiding us through vital roles of all areas of education. There are several books out that explore engagement in education but not as thorough as this. Dr. Vereen's experience and knowledge as educator and parent is unparalleled. I highly recommend this book to all who value the importance of education and its role in our society."

Bridgett Creech
Parent and CEO, RISE Academy

"This book is a clarion call for Educators everywhere to heed the call to action."

Brenda Blunt

CONTENTS

FOREWORD

It is my distinct privilege to write this foreword for my sister, Dr. Deborah M. Vereen's first of many books to come. I am her older sister, Cynthia Vereen-Anderson. I have a Bachelor of Arts degree in Speech Communication with a Public Speaking focus from Edinboro State College (now Edinboro University of Pennsylvania). Additionally, I hold a Master of Arts degree in Human Services Counseling with a Marriage and Family Cognate from Liberty University. I work in hospice, recruiting and training volunteers to either visit terminally ill patients with a life expectancy of six months or less or training volunteers to sit bedside with actively dying patients. When training new volunteers, I tell them "you will likely be the last new friend your patient makes before transitioning form life to death. Do your part to make this friendship a good relationship".

Communicating effectively with others and helping others live as good a life as possible despite personal circumstances, matters deeply to me, not just in my career, but in my personal life as well as I am married with one son.

This book Dr. Deborah Vereen has written will, I believe, forever change the way educators and parents relate to one another for the common good of students everywhere. This book, however, is not just for educators, so if you are not an educator, please know you have located a book written just for you!

Dr. Vereen has coined a phrase "engagement infusion" that I am certain will shake up the world of education if and only if her ideas are implemented by school districts seeking a more modern method to improve the way students are educated. This remarkable book is not just for people who work in or their children attend what are commonly (and unfortunately) called "failing schools". This outstanding work by Dr. Vereen that you are holding in your hands right now, is for people who want to see their community schools shine and impact the entire world for the good of the entire world.

So many schools have gained negative reputations because of the behavior of students. It is not my intention to play any type of "blame game" here, particularly because I am not now, nor have I ever been an educator. How or why so many schools have poor reputations is not nearly as important as how *urgently* the community at large (including residents with no children currently enrolled in school) must find a *solution* to the problem of poorly or underperforming schools.

We no longer have to accept poor, underperforming or failing schools as the norm for the children of our communities; nor do we have to accept poor or no communication or disengagement between teachers, students, administrators, parents and communities. Dr. Vereen outlines a clear path to improving the way our children learn and the way parents, teachers and administrators relate to one another.

This awesome book is like a shining lantern just hung in a darkened room. It dispels nagging questions as if the questions themselves were darkness that administrators and teachers have as to why parents appear unresponsive to their child's educational need. Also addressed is the irritation parents feel when they believe teachers and administrators simply do not care about their child's educational needs. This book represents a much needed and long hoped for paradigm shift in our educational system, if we heed the words of Dr. Vereen.

This work is a result of many years of research, activism, teaching college students, attending as well as speaking at conferences and personal discussions with frustrated parents, teachers and administrators by Dr. Vereen. Her ideas are innovative, invaluable and essential for change in our world as we relate to children.

I have spoken a great deal about how my sister's work can change our educational system. If you are not an educator, please do not allow my preceding words discourage you from reading this book! Here is a brief yet non-exhaustive list of some other professionals who will benefit from this writing: youth mentors, members of law enforcement, social and human services providers, volunteers in school classrooms, faith-based communities, Boy and Girl Scout organizations, pediatric mental and physical health providers, tutors, higher educational policy makers, school board members, recreational center staff, coaches of sports teams and early childhood providers to name a few.

I am very proud of my sister, Dr. Deborah Vereen because anything she does, she does with her entire heart. I can vouch for her love of being an educator and her desire to find new and better ways to help our children learn and mature into teens and adults who make a difference in the world. This book will change the lives of many…beginning with yours.

One of the greatest liabilities of history is that all too many people fail to remain awake through great periods of social change. Every society has its protectors of status quo and its fraternities of the indifferent who are notorious for sleeping through revolutions. Today, our survival depends on our ability to stay awake, to adjust to new ideas, to remain vigilant and to face the challenge of change.

—Dr. Martin Luther King Jr.

Special Acknowledgments

This book, which is my first, is dedicated to these people:

- My parents, Tellie and Jacqueline Vereen, who were my first teachers and my sisters Cynthia Anderson and Brenda Blunt who were my first friends
- My special little friend, Magdalejna Josephina, who will never be forgotten
- The staff at the Ellis School, Jewart's Gymnastics, and Cynthia's School of Dance, who have consistently demonstrated a willingness to collaborate with me in support of my child's growth and development

- My beautifully talented daughter, Jackie, and our beloved Caileigh McDowell, the youngest advocates of parental involvement in the educational process of their children

In loving memory of Caileigh Lynn McDowell
April 11, 1998 – April 2, 2016
The Caileigh Lynn McDowell Foundation
www.caileighsfightsong.com

I thank the following individuals for their professional input as well as for being my professional colleagues and friends:

- Ms. Dawn Golden, Director of Pupil Personnel Services
- Mrs. Agatha Leonard, Education Consultant, Special Education and Pupil Personnel Services
- Mrs. Chardae Seligsohn, Parent and Board of School Director
- Ms. Janet Wilson Carter, Principal

I celebrate and honor the inspirational wisdom of Dr. Sonia Nieto because she has served as a professional role model from afar. She has infused me with interpersonal knowledge through her development of the levels of multicultural education.

Finally, I sincerely thank my eleven-year-old daughter, Jackie, for enthusiastically creating and contributing the original inspiring illustrations.

Who Will Benefit from Reading This Book?

The following adults will benefit from reading this book and from applying the principles outlined in this text relevant to their efforts to positively engage with families as the growth and development of children and young people that they serve are supported:

- Preservice educators and practitioners enrolled in undergraduate and graduate college and university programs, along with students enrolled in human services and social services programs and other relevant fields of study
- Early childhood providers, including but not limited to directors, teachers, and teaching assistants
- Educators from traditional and nontraditional public, vocational, faith-based, independent, and private schools, as well as approved private schools, including district and building-level school administrators, teachers, teaching assistants, central registration personnel, guidance counselors, directors, behavior specialists, school nurses, paraprofessionals, secretaries, athletic coaches, custodial staff, school psychologists, social workers,

food service workers, therapists, security personnel, public relations specialists, ROTC (Reserve Officers' Training Corps) personnel, college placement staff, personal care assistants, and substitute personnel (all educators will benefit from this book whether or not they experience varied levels of challenge with family engagement.)

- Any educator who works valiantly with the highest level of diligence to engage with parents yet maintain a spirit of openness about embracing a new level of knowledge in an effort to increase success in this area

- Early childhood, basic, and higher educational policymakers at the local, state, and federal levels; politicians; lawmakers; and legislators

- Privately hired tutors

- Staff members from tutorial and learning centers

- Board of School Directors representing various types of schools

- Boy Scouts and Girls Scouts organizations

- Various pediatric behavior, mental, and physical health care professionals

- Members of the faith-based community, such as youth group staff, Sunday or Sabbath School and Vacation Bible School workers, and youth pastors and leaders

- Directors, counselors, and staff of various thematic youth camps

- Transportation providers for children and youth

- Volunteers who serve in classrooms, schools, school districts, families, community programs for children and youth, and agencies that interact with the family

- Instructors, coaches, directors, and staff from developmental programs related to the arts and athletics, such as visual and performing arts, competitive and recreational sports groups, clubs, and leagues

- Personnel from youth mentoring programs
- Directors and staff from specialized, academically oriented and/or competitive programs for children and young people, which is inclusive of those with a STEAM (science, technology, engineering, arts, and mathematics) focus
- Staff from recreational centers for children and youth
- Professionals from law enforcement, including training programs, human and social services, and the judiciary who work with children and youth
- Childcare providers and babysitters
- Personnel from early-morning care and after-school programs
- Professionals who provide child-oriented services to families, such as special event and party planners, child photographers, food service workers devoted to attending to youth, employees from amusement and entertainment venues, and activities coordinators at family resorts

Chapter 1

Introduction

In the current era of school reform, educators are professionally obligated to repair what is broken in public education. Instructional efforts must be made to eliminate the achievement gap that has prevailed among historically underperforming students within economically struggling districts, schools, and school districts. In doing so, the list of research-based techniques linked to the very best instructional strategies, along with newly designed programs and protocols that accompany these innovative approaches, have exploded into educational arenas in recent years. Mandated teacher and principal evaluation systems must be implemented with fidelity to increase professional outcomes. Arguments have erupted because positive behavioral interventions and supports have replaced the now seemingly old-fashioned discipline of holding students accountable for their inappropriate actions at school while maintaining a safe learning environment. The lack of adequate funding has forced educators to work harder to produce the expected result of increased student achievement within classrooms filled with more students with a greater depth of need than ever before. Such financial distress is compounded as many traditional public schools now compete with charter and cyber schools. While the list of problematic segments in public education that need to be repaired is robust, I have identified one such focal area in this book.

Whether it is the parent, surrogate parent, a grandparent, aunt, uncle, cousin, older sibling, or even a close family friend, active levels of family engagement is deeply connected to the overall achievement and success of children and young people at every level of basic education. This type of involvement is also applicable to any developmental program or process that a student participates in such as extracurricular activities. Some overt examples follow.

When the family remains involved in their child's educational experiences by developing and maintaining continuous communications with teachers, coaches, administrators, and other school officials, as well as individuals who supervise and guide their development outside of the parameters of school, when they visibly partner with these providers, and when they closely monitor their child's progress, student achievement increases. Such gains in student performance also result when parents maintain a voice in their child's educational programs and when they support the various school- and program-related endeavors of their children. Covert examples that accentuate the link between family engagement and greater student outcomes are shown below.

Families who teach their children at an early age to honor the process of education help them develop foundational skills that will prepare them for the rigors of a successful school experience, and those who serve as their children's first and most significant teachers produce higher-functioning learners. The same is true for families who help their children develop exemplary academic habits. This includes but is not limited to providing a quiet study space, along with adequate educational resources in the home, and developing at-home academic routines like reading each day and participating in educational adventures within the extended community.

Despite the powerful outcomes that result due to overt and covert *family engagement*, some teachers, schools, and school districts are adversely impacted because it is nonfunctioning and nonexistent. For these educators who are consumed with *family disengagement* but still carry the heavy burden of working through some of the aforementioned twenty-first-century educational challenges in an effort to increase student learning outcomes while families remain invisible throughout the educational process of their children, this represents an area in education that I have targeted to repair.

The premise of this book is further substantiated because increased value has been placed upon involving parents and other family members, as well as other primary caregivers as critical partners in the process of education in recent decades. Although the list of research-based and mandated strategies and programs is nearly endless throughout the United States of America, a few concrete examples that demonstrate the importance of these parental involvement efforts are presented here:

- Embedded within the former No Child Left Behind federal legislation of 2002, which was the reauthorized Elementary and Secondary Education Act of 1965, were regulations for the inclusion of parents in the educational process through various means at the school, school district, state, and national level. This included but was not limited to enhanced Title I protocols.
- Grassroots efforts to increase the volume of parental voices continuously emerge as organizations develop to address the need for parents to become active participants throughout specified sectors of the educational process. Community, as well as social activists, politicians, participative parents, and educators, committed to the cause consistently lead these advocacy initiatives.
- Innovative marketing techniques have been employed to promote the use of unique resources strategically designed to promote collaborative parental empowerment between the home, school, and various sectors of the local, regional, national, and global community.
- The Every Student Succeeds Act represents the most recent reauthorized Elementary and Secondary Education Act. As

related to parental involvement, this federal law accentuates all requirements and opportunities for families to be actively engaged with their children's school and school district throughout their educational process at specified levels. More comprehensive Title I and Title III policies are among the enhancements of the law that will increase the efforts of educational entities to engage with families that includes but is not limited to those with low economic resources as well as those who are English learners.

- The United States Department of Education has established national family and community engagement initiatives to strengthen collaborative efforts among schools and school districts. As a result, a protocol called the Dual Capacity-Building Framework for Family–School Partnerships has been created to serve as a research-based blueprint for educational entities to utilize.

My ultimate passion for fostering parental participation and involvement was initiated as I served as family and consumer sciences teacher in public education for thirteen years. I grew to value the important connection between the home and school during this time. Twenty-three additional years of service as Assistant Principal, Principal, Director of Pupil Personnel Services, and Assistant to the Superintendent of Family and Community Engagement and Volunteerism has enabled me to closely analyze the interrelationship between overt and covert family engagement and the quality of student success. As a result, developing meaningful opportunities to involve parents educationally became a part of my unique fingerprint as a public school administrator. My professional epiphany moment was ignited while I served as adjunct professor of multicultural education at the graduate level at two different universities for thirteen years as I also assumed my administrative roles.

I grew to develop a deep appreciation for the research of Dr. Sonia Nieto as it relates to the levels of multicultural education during this time.

In brief, Dr. Nieto outlined specific categories that describe how support for diversity is manifested in schools. These levels include the following:

1. Monoculturalism
2. Tolerance
3. Acceptance
4. Respect
5. Affirmation, Solidarity, and Critique

In an effort to address the problem of parental disengagement relative to the educational experience of their children, I synthesized the Nieto research, along with my broad experiences as practitioner and parent advocate, to create a paradigm shift. This information is introduced by making a correlation between this research and through the acknowledgment that uninvolved, disengaged parents tend to represent multicultural population groups. By establishing a common level of understanding, I classify the following groups of families as multicultural:

1. Families who are economically challenged or are immersed in poverty
2. Those classified as homeless
3. Parents whose religious beliefs may be viewed as radical, as well as those from unpopular or unknown religious groups
4. Individuals considered by educators or society at large as either too young or too old to be a parent

5. Compared to the dominant or most powerful groups within a community, school, or school district, parents from other racial or ethnic groups and those with other linguistic or communication styles, including non-English-speaking people or English learners

6. Those who have nontraditional gender roles and identities

7. Individuals with various mental, physical, and behavioral health conditions and disabilities

8. Transient people groups and those with a migrant status

By combining exclusive elements of my multicultural research primarily based upon the unique research of Dr. Sonia Nieto, by relying on my broad instructional as well as administrative professional experiences, engaging in power of academic reflection, and developing my passion for creating opportunities for families to become educational partners, the model that I have synthesized will empower educators to change their interactions with parents. As a result, the door that leads to increased levels of quality engagement will open wide.

This book is devoted to establishing a sequential framework for developing, nurturing, and sustaining positive family relations within any school environment, church-related provider, extracurricular activity, and other developmental programs so that the goal of student growth and acceleration becomes more of a reality for every person who educates children and young people. While public school educators are the primary audience that I have targeted as the primary beneficiaries of the principles presented in this approach, individuals who have a desire to partner with the families as they work with children and young people to nurture their intellectual, social, emotional, spiritual, and kinesthetic development; unique talents; and special interests would benefit from embracing the strategies that I have outlined.

In an effort to establish a common language associated with the content of this text, the word *family* will primarily be utilized to describe those who function as the primary caregiver of the student, child, or young person. This distinction needs to be made because of the diverse composition of the family structure today. Therefore, family includes the biological, adoptive, or foster parent or parents; anyone who assumes the supervision of the student, such as a biological family member including but not limited to a grandparent, older sibling, aunt, or uncle; and a legal or court-appointed guardian.

Several chapters of this book will conclude with a unique reflective component designed to stimulate deep levels of thinking so that connections will be made between the specific content and the readers who work with children and young people and endeavor to partner with families.

Making Connections

Consider the role that you assume in educating children and young people as you analyze the quote that was spoken by President Barack Obama and shown below:

There is no program and no policy that can substitute for a parent who is involved in their child's education from day one.

1. What is the main idea of this quote?
2. How could you enhance the quality of your educational program by involving parents?
3. What is the relationship between this quote and your profession, *or* what you do to help students grow?
4. How could you design a plan to include families as partners within your instructional setting?
5. What is your opinion about engaging families in your academic, developmental, or spiritual program devoted to educating children and young people? Why?

Chapter 2

The Monocultural Detached Engagement Perspective: A Pile of Debris

The first level of multicultural education developed by Dr. Nieto is monocultural education. She explains the lowest level of her continuum as "a situation in which school structures, policies, curricula, instructional materials, and even pedagogical strategies are primarily representative of only a dominant culture." I extend this definition to also include family engagement. In the monocultural context, an educational leader, teacher, coach, religious instructor, extracurricular advisor, board member, or any other school personnel whose cultural frame of reference is based upon his or her exclusive and/or limited experiences fail to attribute cultural diversity to positivity. Instead, such individuals view diversity as a deficit. Additionally, any professional within any learning environment who celebrates their color-blind disposition fails miserably to distinguish the unique qualities of the individuals they encounter, including family members.

As the adverse impact that monoculturalism has on the development of family partnerships is deeply analyzed in this chapter, it will also be compared to what is known as the self-fulfilling prophecy. Hence, part of the name of this chapter, "A Pile of Debris," is synonymous with the outcome of any educator outcome of any educator who maintains this perspective.

It is difficult for some families from diverse population groups to make genuinely authentic as well as personally meaningful connections with those who educate their children while sustaining a monocultural point of view. Unfortunately, such adverse monocultural tendencies breed disengagement because families become disenfranchised, disconnected, and disillusioned with the entire educational process involving their children.

A critique of the troubling characteristics of monocultural educators follows:

- These individuals tend to be overtly and covertly domineering and exercise power and control over multicultural families.
- Coldness, indifference, and insensitivity, along with an attitude that emanates superiority, manifest during verbal and nonverbal interactions and encounters with families who are different than the monocultural educational provider.
- Efforts to relate to as well as communicate and bond with multicultural families are artificial and insincere.
- Such school personnel believe that the multicultural family is inferior.

According to the self-fulfilling prophecy, which will be closely examined in the next chapter, the internal beliefs that an individual maintains about those that they encounter and interact with will ultimately manifest in their actions toward them. In more poignant terms, monocultural personnel will treat multicultural parents according to their beliefs that they have about them.

Unfortunately, these adverse and troubling yet negative monocultural attributes produce disturbing results for the schools that desperately need family support and active levels of family involvement. These terrible consequences include the following:

Detached families who do not have the intrinsic or extrinsic will to partner with the school

Embarrassing responses to irrelevant, insincere, and superficial attempts for educational entities to form relationships with families

Blame placed upon families by educational officials for not being actively engaged in the process of education at home and at school

Resentful families for not being viewed by the school as capable of being an educational partner

Invisible families who remain unknown to teachers, administrators, and other instructional providers

Severed relations between families and the school

Therefore, it is extremely critical for those responsible for delivering any type of educational services to children and young people to abandon this unsettling monocultural perspective so that the process of fostering healthy levels of family participation will be conceived and built in a seamless manner. Doing so involves building capacity to move through the higher segments of the Nieto continuum.

Parental Interview

Understanding the Adverse Impact of a Monocultural Perspective within an Educational Setting

1. Has a teacher or any other educational provider made you feel like you did not measure up to his or her expectations as you worked to engage with those within the learning environment for the benefit of your child because you were different from him or her? (Perhaps you were from a different racial or ethnic group.)

    Yes. I am an African American woman who works in the school district that my child attends. Even though I am always easily accessible and very involved as a parent, a terrible situation happened to me that caused me to feel like I was not valued as both a family and a professional colleague. I felt because the individuals involved in the incident were white that they utilized their authority and power to make me and my child degraded. I especially felt that they deliberately put me in a position of being subservient to them so that I understood my true position compared to them.

2. Explain the circumstances.

    Before I get into the explanation, I must start by saying in no way do I condone fighting, physical aggression, or violence of any way.

I also believe that any child has a breaking point, and no matter how much talking and coaching they receive, they have the potential to make a bad choice.

With that being said, my child was involved in an incident—a physical fight with another student. The initiator had a history of bullying my child despite the consequences given by the school and regardless of my child's attempts to ignore the student. The incident reached a peak when a very brief physical altercation erupted. My child sent a text message to me to let me know of the incident. Unfortunately, I did not hear from anyone connected with the school for until almost an hour later. There were several concerns that I had with the situation that my child was involved in.

The first concern is how I was officially informed of the situation. While I was at a professional meeting with others, a school administrator involved with the case sent a text message to a colleague about the incident. The colleague publically announced the incident to me as other professionals heard it at the same time that I did. I felt as though the individual who announced the incident did so in a mocking manner to discredit me. At that point, I not only felt embarrassed as the parent and a professional colleague, but I also felt like the rights of my child were violated.

The second concern I had with the occurrence was the manner in which it was documented. When I received a copy of the disciplinary notice, the school administrator noted that I was informed of the incident by way of telephone even though I was never notified. This was clearly not true as the school official did not contact me at all. Even though a security film captured the event and did not show my child engaging in any act of physical aggression, disciplinary consequences were administered to my child. My child now has a discipline record for just being present when the other student fought my. I instantly began to think if this was the way I was being treated as a parent and employee, I can only imagine how other parents were treated.

The third concern is that my child received a formal citation for the incident. While I know this happens with most fights, I also know it is at the discretion of the principal whether or not a student should be cited. The principal chose to do so with my child despite the evidence that was gathered to prove that my child did not exchange physical blows.

The final concern is that my child and I were made to feel like criminals while attending a hearing with the local magistrate despite the fact that my child did no wrong.

3. What was the role of the educator?

The educators involved were school administrators.

4. As a parent, how did that situation make you feel?

When I think about monoculturalism, it speaks to cultural superiority. The incident proved to me that even though I am a professional African American female, the school administrator from the school treated me as though I was less than they were because they devalued me as not only a professional but also a colleague. The will of the administrator to control the situation and to ignore evidence, truth, and my petitions on behalf of my child prevailed. This has devastated me.

5. Do you believe the educator devalued you because he or she considered you to be unworthy of being an equal partner?

Yes. As a parent, I had no one to turn to as I tried to express my concerns. As it can be imagined, this incident has left bitterness in my heart regarding the inability of the school to treat me as an equal partner who has a voice as well as the right to be treated fairly. If I was a valued member of the school community, I would have been treated in a respectful manner. They would have also valued my concerns, and the outcome of the incident would have been different for me and my child.

6. What message do you have for any educational providers who consider themselves superior to any multicultural (differences according to culture; race; ethnicity; religion; gender identity; economic status; behavioral, mental, or physical health diagnosis; and so on) parent?

Since the administration used their power to suppress me and my child, it is important for such educators to know that as a parent who is involved in my child's education, I will exercise my right to school choice. Educators need to know that there are other schools that care about not offending and harming those who are different from those who are in control of schools. Principals, teachers, and everyone else who work in schools need to know that student enrollment will suffer when they are the cause of families suffering needlessly. I will be placing my child in another educational institution that will be able to meet their social, emotional, and academic needs. I will not tolerate having my African American child lumped into a category of being labeled as a disruptive thug and receiving the harshest form of punishment possible from the school because of their race.

Chapter 3

Tolerance: Aloof, Spiritless Engagement

This chapter thoroughly examines the impact of a term, which has grown to become widely popularized and celebrated in educational circles as well as within other sectors of society, has on the efforts of institutions of learning to successfully partner with families.

Tolerance is the next level of the multicultural education continuum constructed by Sonia Nieto. It represents the initial attempt of acknowledging the pluralistic characteristics of other human beings. According to Nieto, "To be tolerant means to have the capacity to bear something although at times it may be unpleasant, and to tolerate differences means to endure them although not necessarily to embrace them."

To expand the meaning of tolerance, it also means to put up with something. Additionally, to tolerate something accentuates a level of discomfort. Nieto further considers tolerance as a "distasteful acceptance" because this level of support for multicultural education stands on shaky ground because what is tolerated today can too easily be rejected tomorrow. While there has been an increase in promoting "tolerance for diversity" over the years, according to Dr. Nieto, it reflects an inadequate expression of support and does not go far enough.

Even though tolerance is misrepresented as an admirable characteristic that encompasses a healthy component of cultural relevance and acceptance, I will analyze the dangerous outcomes that this derogatory act produces.

Individuals may not be able to articulate the realization that they have when another person, group of people, or an established organization merely endures their personhood or presence. In addition, such people who are victimized by being distastefully accepted may not have developed a defensive voice, which protects them from the unsettling effects of this maltreatment. However, the inner spirit of tolerated people breaks when they encounter those who feign acceptance and respect. Most damaging, those who tolerate others erect barriers of isolation, suspicion, inferiority, resentment, anger, and distrust. Ultimately, the impact of tolerance on the development of reciprocated positive family and school partnerships is devastating because four negative outcomes prevail:

1. *The obstruction of positive relationship building.* There is an alarming tendency of the overt behaviors of those who tolerate the family yet work with or supervise the development of their children to block authentic relationship-building efforts. The interpersonal qualities of educational providers who merely endure that family include demeaning overt tendencies, like instigating verbal power struggles, along with verbally communicating in a manner that manifests a level of entitlement and their personally perceived superiority. The latter is commonly known as talking down to the family among some cultural groups. Family members are adversely impacted by these and other derogatory behaviors will both retreat and avoid professional interactions with the educator. Anger will encompass other families. Unfortunately, this very powerful emotion will prevent the possibility of the establishment of any type of relationship. Another consequence is that savvy parents who know how to access community-based services and supports may opt to collaborate with advocates as they endeavor to work with educators who tolerate them. Such drastic measures will provide impacted families with assurances that their voices

are being heard. However, in doing so, relationship-building attempts become too damaged to be repaired. Finally, tolerated families become so dissatisfied that they have not made an interpersonal connection with the educators that they severe ties with the learning institution by removing their child from the educational facility or program because of the deep level of damage perpetuated by the tolerant school district, teachers, and so on.

2. *The manifestation of the self-fulfilling prophecy.* In 1948, sociologist Robert Merton established the term *self-fulfilling prophecy* to articulate the belief that one's beliefs, expectations, and attitudes about others will be influenced by the way they interact with and treat a person or designated group of people. Consequently, those interactions and overall treatment will cause the targeted person or group to behave or react as expected. This theory is put into the context of educational providers who only tolerate the families that they are supposed to serve and support. When such educators maintain an unhealthy, inaccurate, and derogatory perspective about families different from the societal group that the professional represents, their attitude mirrors their opinion about them. These educators have a tendency to possess a crude and unrefined disposition while working and interacting with the families they tolerate. Overall, the approach of these educators tends to be harsh. Unfortunately, the spontaneous reaction and behavior of the family that has been tolerated will become very consistent with the way that such professionals treated them.

3. *The communication of adverse nonverbal messages.* Individuals who assume the responsibility of supporting the growth and development of learners but tolerate the family communicate

very specific, unacceptable, and inappropriate nonverbal messages. The subtle transfer of such information discourages families from establishing meaningful partnerships with educational entities. A list of these unspoken derogatory signals and messages initiated by the educator follows:

- Avoiding the use of smiles or other facial characteristics that reflect a pleasant personality
- Failing to initiate the use of or sustaining good eye contact during interactive encounters
- Reacting to the physical touch of a family member like a handshake in a distasteful manner that reflects disdain and disgust as well as the fear of contamination
- Using proxemics to establish broad and deliberate professional boundaries away from family members during verbal interactions with them
- Utilizing gestures that emphasize the emotional state of nervousness, anger, indifference, frustration, and anxiety along with boredom, including but not limited to keeping the arms folded across the chest and nail biting during any verbal discourse
- The inappropriate use of voice quality during verbal discourse with a family member by either using a loud, commanding, or harsh tone like shouting or using the voice in a condescending or patronizing manner such as exaggerated enunciation, again, with increased volume, in an effort to try to enable the family to comprehend what is being stated

4. *A superior disposition prevails.* Educational providers who merely tolerate the personhood of any family that they are supposed to serve exercise power over them. This dominance manifests through attitudes, behaviors, and the verbalizations of the educators.

- The attitude of tolerant educators mirrors the covert belief about the status of the family. While these opinions are nontransparent and invisible to the observer, such families are secretly judged as unequal and inferior.
- The behavior of tolerant educators who exude power includes negative overt responses to family members, which are undisguised, visible, and blatant. Some of these exhibited behaviors include criticism, aggression, and manipulation.
- The verbal initiation made to families by an educator who tolerates them and considers him or herself to be more superior will be harsh as well as demeaning. Additionally, such families will feel as though they are being ridiculed as they are being spoken to in a challenging and argumentative manner. Ultimately, the verbal encounter may cause the family to feel less than intelligent.

Many individuals throughout varied sectors of society remain deeply passionate about the notion of tolerance. Such people promote their enthusiasm for their tolerant perspective that they wholeheartedly embrace by celebrating their efforts in being a culturally sensitive human being. Unfortunately, because of the mere definition associated with the act of tolerating another person or people group, this concept breeds negativity.

The devastating reality is that it is impossible for educational providers who endure and put up with any family member to work with them in a mutually cooperative manner. Public as well as private school teachers; day care providers; religious instructors; school administrators; coaches; behavior, mental, and physical health providers; board of school directors, along with policy makers—*the list is endless*—must develop and sustain positive relationships with families to ensure the healthy progressive growth of the learners that they provide services for.

Tolerance must be avoided within any educational or developmental context.

Just remember, that whatever you put up with you end up with.
(Unknown)

Tolerance

A Journal Entry from the Heart of a Mother

Dear Diary,

Simply being *tolerated* is not a great feeling. In fact, it is a terrible feeling. I should know how bad it makes you feel because of how I felt when I attended a meeting at school regarding my children.

I remember walking into the meeting room a few minutes early and instantly feeling unwelcome. Teachers and other school officials were already seated. No one spoke to me or even acknowledged my presence. As I sat in a chair without anyone actually inviting me to take a seat, my ears perked up as a side conversation ignited among the other early attendees. I looked up to make contact with the others in the room who were talking. They ignored me and never invited me to join the conversation. Unbothered by my gaze, their conversation continued and grew louder. These seemingly professional people did not seem very professional anymore because their conversation was filled with subtle yet callous remarks about me even though I was sitting right there. Their sly facial expressions were directed toward me. I was shocked! I wondered what I did wrong. I began questioning myself with what did I do wrong. Why didn't these people like me? Did I have on the wrong clothes? Is it the color of my skin? Since I am a young parent, I even began to wonder if it was my age. Once the meeting formally started, the chatter ended. However, the sly facial expressions and the passive-aggressive body language continued.

I felt very, very sad because my presence was being tolerated. I was not respected as a member of the school team because I wasn't a part of the group. I was being ignored. Even though the meeting was about my children, I was excluded.

Despite everything that took place before and during the meeting, my sadness turned into determination. I decided that I was not going to let someone else's insecurities and unprofessionalism intimidate me. After all, I was there for my children, and nobody will *ever* scare me away from ensuring their safety or security.

I really hope that my next entry will be about how the school respected me.

Until next time!

Chapter 4

Reviving Family Engagement
through Acceptance

Acceptance is the next segment of the multicultural education continuum developed by Dr. Nieto, which is also equated with the level of family engagement. In the context of fostering and sustaining positive levels of family engagement, which ultimately benefits students being supported by contributing to their overall success, this level accentuates the role of educational providers as well as the schools and school districts along with individuals who support the development of children and young people in accepting realities of who the families really are that they are obligated to serve. This level is much more favorable compared to the monocultural and tolerance components that were previously explored.

Acceptance is a willful act of approval that overrides any diverse characteristic exemplified by any family compared to the characteristics of members of dominant groups who work with students that some who exist at the tolerant level were prone to disrespect. As a result, the family encounters approval as they interact and engage with school personnel regardless of their economic status, religious beliefs, interpersonal nuances, gender identity, clothing style or decorative adornments worn or displayed on the body, race or ethnicity, behavior, mental or physical health diagnosis, linguistic patterns, or any other difference they may display.

The power of acceptance outweighs the notion of tolerance, which was thoroughly elaborated on in the last chapter. Unlike the attitudes and behaviors aligned with merely putting up with the families of learners, acceptance embraces the dignity of each member of a family by validating their personhood. Educators who accept each family possess endearing personality traits that breed healthy levels of reciprocated collaboration.

To further magnify the perspective of this engagement level, the building blocks of acceptance have been developed to provide a concrete analysis of this area. Each will be elaborated on.

Acceptance Building Block Number 1

Acknowledge the Individuality
of Each Family

Teachers, guidance counselors, coaches, board members, and other educational providers and child trainers who accept the families that they work with value their distinctive characteristics. This enables every family to be noticed and considered to be uniquely one of a kind and not rejected because of this. Whether from dominant or diverse populations or less dominant groups, whether eccentric or conservative, or whether extraverted and verbose or socially withdrawn, such families are embraced.

Acceptance Building Block Number 2

Avoid Making Comparisons

Also, deeply rooted in building block number 1 is the second component. Families who are accepted are not compared to other families. Just as it is an unacceptable practice for educators to compare siblings or other groups of children, it is equally wrong to do so with parents. Even though some families may possess similar biological characteristics—such as belonging to the same race, coming from similar economic backgrounds as evidenced the identifiable factors like the neighborhood that they reside in, their capacity to maintain parallel lifestyles, or their overt display of other likenesses—it is unfair to categorize family units as being one and the same. Furthermore, such comparisons open the door to various forms of social injustices, like bigotry, discrimination, stereotyping, xenophobia, prejudice, racial profiling, and so on. Acceptance confirms the personhood or the unique composition of each family in an individualized, separate manner.

Acceptance Building Block Number 3

Maintain a Nonjudgmental Engagement Approach

The last acceptance building block emphasizes the importance of educational providers remaining nonjudgmental while interacting with families during verbal, nonverbal, and written exchanges. Maintaining a judgment disposition is consistent with sustaining beliefs and opinions about any family without an authentic explanation or concrete proof. Doing so also represents one of the highest forms of discrimination because it creates blatant opportunities for the infestation of bigotry, stereotyping, inequality, inequity, and prejudice, as well as other deeper forms of injustices. The consequence of this is that it alienates the family and also radically grows resentment, hostility, and anger. The final building block of acceptance destroys preconceived attitudes and beliefs about any family that school personnel serve by promoting a spirit of cooperation and mutual trust. Furthermore, this building block reinforces the importance of educators remaining committed to understanding each family on an individual basis.

As the analysis of acceptance concludes, sentimental reflections are evoked as the following quotes are thoughtfully considered:

The Serenity Prayer

God grant me the serenity to accept the things that I cannot change; Courage to change the things I can; And the wisdom to know the difference. (Reinhold Niebuhr)

Accept then act. Whatever the present moment contains, accept it as you had chosen it. Always work with it, not against it. (Eckhart Tolle)

What is projected is verbally in your heart. (Agatha Leonard)

Nothing brings down walls as surely as acceptance. (Deepak Chopra)

Have a big enough heart to love unconditionally and a broad enough mind to embrace the differences that make each of us unique. (D. B. Harop)

Go and love someone unconditionally exactly the way they are. And then watch how quickly they transform into the greatest, truest version of themselves. When one feels seen and appreciated in their own essence, one is instantly empowered. (Wes Angelozzi)

As the meaningful quotes have been considered, the discussion of acceptance is succinctly summarized in the acronym that follows.

Approval

Confirm

Cooperate

Endorse

Personify

Trust

Acknowledge

Notice

Concede

Embrace

Compared to maintaining a narrow coupled with a damaging monocultural perspective and one that perpetuates attitudes, beliefs, and behaviors associated with tolerance, the idea of acceptance is a more appropriate interpersonal approach for school personnel to maintain with families.

The next chapter will describe a more profound level of family engagement.

Acceptance

An Authentic Observation from a Parent

I am writing this observation from a parent's perspective. This narrative speaks to the topic of *acceptance* and what I view that to look like from my perspective. My focus will be on my experience as a parent of a newly identified special education student.

I find it imperative to provide background information to paint the picture of my experience regarding an educator who made a profound difference in the life and school experience of my daughter and our family.

Thirty years ago in a small town of Abbeville, Louisiana, my husband and I were blessed with a beautiful baby girl. She arrived at twenty-eight gestational weeks. Needless to say, she arrived far too early in life. Because of this, our child faced many, many challenges. In addition, she had to undergo six surgeries in her early childhood years. It was clear early on that she would also have developmental challenges. Most of the typical developmental milestones were reached far beyond the predictable scales. The first three years with our daughter were trying times and put a lot of strain on our marriage.

When my child was a little over three years old, our family moved from Louisiana to Southfield, Michigan, in pursuit of a better opportunity through my husband's employment. This was a difficult adjustment for our entire family. Besides a major cultural shock, the weather was shocking in that we experienced our first bout with snow—and a lot of it! Since our daughter was still not school-age, we put her in a popularly known and reputable early childhood facility. (This program still exists today as an option for parents and children from birth through school-aged as well as beyond.) Regarding acceptance, the staff and daily programming were absolutely outstanding. This was the gateway into a formalized school experience for my child. My husband and I felt extremely accepted, and the staff valued our input, needs, history, and background. They accepted us as individuals. They took our daughter's initial educational experience very seriously. This was indeed one of the most positive experiences for us because of the inclusive practices that were implemented and incorporated. We were touched by the natural theme of mutual respect between the center providers and ourselves. Soon thereafter, we had our son—our second child. Both of our children reaped full benefit of being placed in an environment that was so accepting and sensitive of their cultural, ethnic, geographic, and educational needs.

By the time my daughter was ready for traditional school, her social emotional foundation was built because of placing her in an inclusive, sensitive, competent, and accepting environment. Socially and emotionally, my daughter appeared to adapt rather quickly as she had many friends and was an active participant in many enrichment activities. However, she appeared to struggle academically.

To fast forward to her kindergarten year, my little girl's teacher recommended that she repeat her kindergarten year to allow her to catch up to her so-called typically developing peers. As a parent, I felt very overwhelmed in making this decision. At the time, I was not as astute as many parents are today with regard to seeking outside support and resources for children with disabilities. Now I also question whether those resources existed to the degree that they exist today. Our decision, once we weighed the pros and cons, concluded that we would agree to this teacher's recommendation and have our five-year-old repeat her kindergarten year. I continued to second-guess myself by wondering if this was the best decision that I could have made.

As the years advanced, my daughter continued to struggle in her academic endeavors as an early learner in elementary school. It was around her fourth-grade year that we decided to pursue special education services by requesting a formal evaluation for our daughter. My daughter was tested and qualified for these services. She was declared a student with a specific learning disability primarily in the area of mathematics computation and also written expression. My child received her first IEP (Individualized Educational Program). Once she qualified to receive these specialized services, she was assigned a special education case manager who was the resource room teacher. This was a huge turning point for our daughter and our family.

I was extremely frustrated with what I viewed to be my daughter's lack of concrete progress, along with the difficulties that came with having a child with a disability. To be honest, at this particular point and time in my life, my frustration was at a breaking point. Being an educator myself, my standards of expectation have always been extremely high with regard to what I think my children should achieve.

We had moved again from a very comfortable neighborhood, which met all our social needs. In doing so, we left a diverse school district and moved into a community and school district, which comprised of less than 1 percent African American residents and students. We were now a part of a population that wanted part of the so-called American dream. In order to achieve that, we had to go to the outskirts of our diverse neighborhood into a very segregated neighborhood. I did not mention that we were an African American family earlier in this narrative because I did not recognize the validity of mentioning our race or ethnicity until now.

There were natural challenges in that the school district was comprised of less than 1 percent African American students. I will not elaborate specifically on some of those challenges. However, as an African American woman, sometimes there is a tendency to question whether things are occurring or conversely not occurring due to one's race and ethnicity. Despite my questions, our daughter and younger son seemed to be well adapted to their new school district. They both made friends and did very well socially. However, my daughter continued to struggle academically.

I found myself attending her IEP meetings in a very closed, suspicious, and defensive mind-set. The teacher asked to discuss my daughter's progress or what I perceived to be a lack of progress and also asked if she could make a *home visit* and speak with me in person. Initially, I hesitated because by nature, I am an extremely private person. I did not eagerly want to open my house up to a teacher whom I did not know, as well either. After a lot of thought about this, and as a result of multiple discussions with my husband, I decided to invite the teacher into my home for the meeting. This was the turning point in my daughter's academic success because her teacher confronted me about my disposition. This professional pointed out her observations about my negative and defensive positioning in my very own kitchen at my house. It was not until the teacher brought to my attention her frustration in working with my daughter and always feeling that I was uncooperative that I realized that I needed to change, even though I have always been a very direct person. (Thirty years ago, I would also guess that being very young, perhaps immature, certainly unpolished, and not as informed as I am today, my attitude was the way it was.) As a result of having a very candid conversation with the teacher right in my home, I was able to take a moment and evaluate this entire situation. I was able to be honest with myself and came to terms with what I initially viewed to be a very unfair and even tragic situation because I had a child with a disability. I credited the teacher for helping me to come to the realization that my child had potential to be as successful as any other student. I also came to the realization that I needed to get out of my child's way and allow her to grow. Additionally, I came to the realization that I needed to entrust my daughter's education to caring, compassionate, and competent educators such as the one described above.

To fast forward my story to the present time, the value of a home visit is unmeasured. It is the one critical act that can certainly bridge any gap that may exist between families and home because it demonstrates the total acceptance of a teacher. As a result of my daughter's story, I have learned that acceptance is a reciprocated standard to achieve, although it may have a different meaning based upon an individual's unique experiences, background, belief system, and moral compass. Acceptance should never be underestimated as a means to advance any and all educational goals that exist between schools and home. I am now more accepting of the importance of my role in being my child's strongest ally and advocate. I am more accepting of the role that the education community plays in the lives of students too. Finally, while my daughter is an adult, I am accepting of her role in her own development.

Chapter 5

Respect Inspires and Stimulates Engagement

Respect is the next level of multicultural education outlined within the Nieto schema. Again, in the context of this book, each level is equated to the stages of family engagement that those who assume the responsibility of educating and developing children and youth must endeavor to both avoid and achieve to build the capacity for a healthy partnership to be sustained.

Simply stated, Sonia Nieto explains that "respect means to admire and hold in high esteem." Because of the power of this definition, respect is the most desirable level of family engagement presented thus far.

Respect is equated to the adhesive that strengthens the bond between the three building blocks of acceptance explained in the last chapter. Because respect represents a rich multidimensional approach to meaningfully engage with families, each aspect of this level will be illuminated in this section.

First of all, respect is established when educational personnel develop a high opinion about the family paired with a high regard for them. This engagement approach is strength-based because the parents and caregivers are revered as resilient and resourceful, as well as impactful partners who are deeply connected and invested in the developmental process of their children. Therefore, teachers, mentors, coaches, and others committed to fostering the growth of learners do not view the family or their collaborations or their active levels of involvement within the instructional environment as a deficit, threat, liability, or hindrance.

Secondly, the educator-family professional relationship is reinforced because of the infusion of the character elements of honor and values that are initiated by the school. The family is esteemed with pride and joy, and their collaborative efforts are treasured and genuinely appreciated.

Next, family engagement efforts are fortified by the welcome that is received by educators when they participate in the learning process at any level at any time. The reaction of those who deliver the education to children and young people always radiate with a happy disposition when respect is embedded into their approving demeanor.

In addition, respect is solidified among parents when educators advocate for the best interests for the benefit of the learners they serve. This type of respect is reinforced when families are defended by educational personnel when other educators oppose their collaborative tendencies and endeavors. In essence, such respectful instructional providers champion parents, guardians, and caregivers because they stand up for them as these educators bolster collegial partnerships.

Finally, respect manifests when the school supports the family by providing various types of assistance. Such help includes but is not limited to connecting them to the designated resources that they may require and incorporating specific strategies that will both strengthen and stabilize the development of the learner. Responding to parental questions and concerns with a spirit of fidelity in a timely manner also provides help to them.

The broad dimensions of respect embedded in the demeanor of educational policy makers, school personnel, and those who deliver educational services become synthesized into meaningful levels of family engagement. Despite this favorable outcome, the absolute highest level of engagement will be evaluated in the chapter that follows.

Dignity

Dignity is the ability to stand strong and tall in the face of adversity while being able to bow to the elderly and crawl with the children.

Dignity is taking a stand for your beliefs without closing your mind to another's opinion.

Dignity is being an example by your deeds and through your words, avoiding gossip, anger, and lies.

Dignity will manifest itself in the warmth of your smile, the depth of your love, and kindness for your fellowman.

(Mychal Wynn)

A Narrative from a Parent

Respect Made a Difference for Me

My daughter received gifted support services when she was enrolled in high school. There were four teachers who worked beyond my expectations as they provided specialized instruction. Their assistance extended not only to my child but also to all the other students. I can vividly recall how loving, genuinely interested, and academically challenging they were toward my daughter. Each of the teachers always kept me informed about my daughter's progress. They also let me know when they thought she was slacking at not doing her best. Of course, my daughter did not care for my constant communications with these teachers at the time. However, eleven years later, she definitely appreciates what we did for her. What made a difference for me as a parent? I never had to second-guess whether my daughter had the best academic experience possible because the teachers respected me as well as my need to remain informed about her performance. I can now see the fruits of her teachers' labors. So does my daughter.

Chapter 6

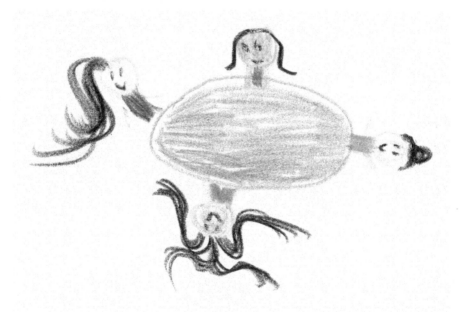

Affirmation, Solidarity, and Critique Ignites and Accelerates Engagement

The final level of multicultural education prescribed by Dr. Nieto that has been translated into the last level of family engagement is the affirmation, solidarity, and critique component. As Nieto believes, this is the most challenging level of multicultural education to accomplish, and to me, it is the most difficult level of family engagement to achieve.

Because the thrust of this book is devoted to building and supporting positive relations and interactions between parents and guardians, along with those who assume the responsibility for facilitating the development of their children, I will thoroughly define each segment of this final level according to this context. Most significantly, I will elaborate on this component by synthesizing the key concepts to make it applicable to the intensive analysis of family engagement.

Affirmation

Affirmation, the first part of this level, refers to the affective, emotional acknowledgment, encouragement, and support genuinely initiated by the educational provider that is authentically extended to the family.

I developed affirmation descriptors to epitomize the complexity of this profound state of engagement. Each segment outlined below represents a strategic dimension of each concept that is revealed by analyzing each layer of affirmation.

Affirmation Descriptors

1. *Compassion.* The heart and soul of affirmation is compassion. This refers to the sympathy that educators must have for families that they believe that they are predestined to serve. Compassion is also inclusive of remaining sensitive to the needs of parents and guardians when they seek support in securing various levels of help for their child. Consideration is also evidenced through compassion. Ultimately, when compassion exists, parents are apt to bond with teachers.

2. *Empathy.* The next layer of affirmation is empathy. This professional character trait develops the capacity of educators to truly understand the life situation of families. Empathy manifests when various instructors, school personnel, and others affiliated with the learning process make a concentrated effort to get to know their families to their unique differences

and individual characteristics. Empathy also mirrors reciprocity because educators reveal parts of themselves, including but not limited to their educational, cultural, and family background, to parents. Thus, this trait opens the door to interpersonal transparency, which builds the trust that is required to develop a legitimate partnership for the benefit of the overall growth of the student.

3. *Love and Care.* Love and care is the third segment of affirmation. This affective component deals with the feelings and emotional status educators maintain as they participate in engagement endeavors with families. The verbal interactions initiated by the professional reflect concern because they are made with kindness and respect. Nonverbal interactions also radiate these humanistic character traits. Since school personnel maintain a nurturing demeanor at this level, they position themselves to mentor families who would benefit from interpersonal guidance and reassurance. Educators who reflect love and care create a sense of security and positive well-being that result in parents along with caregivers being comfortable within all phases of the learning environment, as well as during encounters with those who direct the learning process. The positive emotions that emerge at this level are unconditional and authentic.

4. *Encouragement.* The encouragement affirmation descriptor is an inspirational and spiritual component. Educators functioning at this level use spoken and unspoken types of positive reinforcement to impart hope to the families they serve. Examples of these may include telling a parent something as simple as "everything is going to be fine" or by giving a reassuring touch on the arm or shoulder during a verbal exchange. Additionally, if a close professional partnership already exists, the educator who is

encouraging may initiate a hug. A higher level of this descriptor includes maintaining optimism during parental interactions. Such inspiring teachers help the family acquire the ability to envision their future, as well as the future of their children filled with promise. Finally, coaches, instructors, and all the others who guide the development of students celebrate the strength of the children and young people they mentor, supervise, and so on with passion.

5. *Motivation.* The final descriptor is motivation. This segment is extremely impactful because every other affirmation descriptor energizes it. Ultimately, educators at this level stimulate the development of parental intrinsic motivation. This intrapersonal motivation propels the family to support the education of their children with fervor as their collaborative endeavors with those who provide instruction remain powerfully seamless and unstoppable. Because of this, parents embrace the extrinsic rewards associated with their children achieving and performing at extremely high levels compared to learners who achieve and perform at lower levels due to family disengagement.

While the extremely dynamic and spirited affirmation engagement component has been thoroughly detailed so that all the parts have been distinguished, the next segment of this level that accompanies it will be explored.

Solidarity

My definition of solidarity is analogous to family engagement endeavors. Straightforwardly, *solidarity* refers to educators working together with parents harmoniously for the common purpose of affirming families.

Once the education providers establish and maintain affirming relationships with parents and caregivers that they serve by manifesting the descriptor characteristics that have been systematically interpreted, a number of variables must be evidenced within the learning environment.

First of all, any teacher, coach, or other educator who welcomes affirmation as he or she partners with families must surround him or herself with colleagues who share an identical engagement perspective. The popularized quote by an unknown author, which reads "there is power in numbers," accentuates the role empowerment plays when like-minded professionals form an alliance. Consistently working with another as a cooperative union to advance the notion of affirmation generates momentum within a learning environment and ultimately leads to the next positive outcome.

Secondly, solidarity is demonstrated through the team spirit that emerges as professionals unite for the cause of affirmation within their educational setting. Once colleagues recognize the compelling result of extremely high levels of engagement when each family is accepted, respected, and most significantly affirmed by educators, harmony grows.

Finally, the concept of solidarity is strengthened when individuals responsible for the development of children and young people possess an authentic amount of dedication as they work together as a cohesive unit to allow affirmation to remain a priority as well as the norm.

Because of the tremendous value placed upon affirmation, it permeates the professional atmosphere of any learning center or school. This propels teams of educators and other professionals to willfully and enthusiastically embrace the final part of the affirmation, solidarity, and critique family engagement component to be activated.

Critique

My explanation of this idea continues to remain consistent with family engagement.

It is vital for educators to regularly invest in professional time to reflect upon their engagement efforts as it relates to the full integration of all facets of affirmation relevant to performing duties with a spirit of solidarity. This thought-provoking process facilitates the deliberation of efforts made in this area. Giving deep consideration to this collective process also helps identify deficits in the course of action that has been taken. Most importantly, accumulating and analyzing uniquely designed formative, summative, and qualitative family engagement data sets will provide the educators with reliable and valid information about the actual progress. Once it has been discovered that the cohesive team of educators has made a reasonable amount of growth through a careful examination of the family engagement efforts at this complex level, opportunities must be developed to acknowledge as well as commemorate the success of this collegial approach. However, if a judgment is made regarding shortcomings or complete failures in the unified protocols of family engagement, the educators working together in unison should become more determined to make improvements at this phase of parental involvement.

In conclusion, "affirmation, solidarity, and critique" component is the most dominant, powerful, and compelling level of family engagement. As a result, its prominence in formulating strong partnerships between educational providers and the families they serve, this level is synonymous with the cornerstone of the engagement process. That means that this robust segment effectively supports every dimension of each affirmation descriptor as well as every component of solidarity and critique. While it is the most challenging engagement level to achieve, the professional character traits that are authentically created when educators interact with families at this segment are interrelated. Thus, the strong relationships that result are created due to the establishment of the team spirit.

The following quotes celebrate the sovereignty of bond that is established between schools and families at this engagement level:

> Unity is strength. When there is teamwork and collaboration, wonderful things can be achieved. (Mattie J. T. Spepanek)

> The deepest level of communication is not communication, but communion. It is wordless . . . beyond speech . . . beyond concept. (Thomas Merton)

> I offer you peace. I offer you love. I offer you friendship. I see your beauty. I hear your need, I feel your feelings. My wisdom flows from the Highest/source. I salute that source in you. Let us work together for unity and love. (Mahatma Gandhi)

> Being involved in the well-being and advancement of one's own community is a most natural thing to do. (Clarence Clemons)

> There is no better place to create a community of caring than in our schools—the heart of our future. (Patricia Gándara)

Professional Team Meeting Template

Example of Personal Reflection

    I.   How well am I integrating the affirmation descriptors in my interactions with our families?

   II.   How well are we integrating the affirmation descriptors in our interactions with our families?

Example of Solidarity

  III. Sharing Session

       A. Discuss your perspective with a partner and then with your department or a larger group of colleagues.

       B. Participate in a whole group-sharing session.

Example of Critique

  IV. Evaluating Our Progress

       A. Formulate an opinion about our collective growth in this area.

       B. How can we improve as a team?

       C. What will the improvement indicators be?

Chapter 7

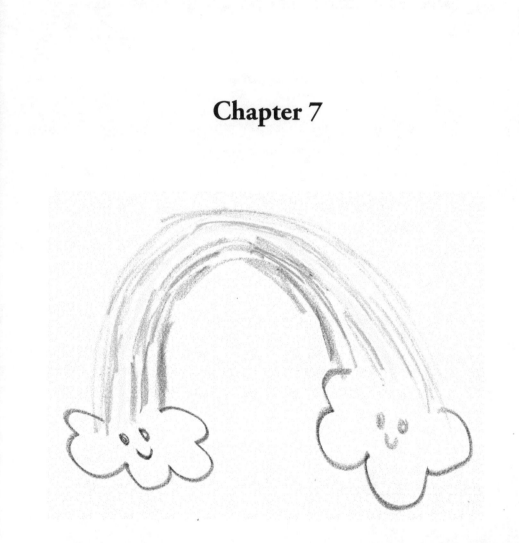

Engagement Fusion Is
Electrified Engagement

As analyzed and differentiated in earlier chapters, the monocultural and tolerance levels of family engagement are extremely detrimental to the establishment of positive interactions and relationships. Both adverse segments embedded in the multicultural education continuum developed by Nieto prevents school district, policy makers, and educational personnel, as well as those responsible for facilitating the growth and development of students from establishing a meaningful mutual partnership for the betterment of the overall success of learners and the inclusive process of education. Therefore, these perspectives, which I refer to as negative, must not be embraced. More concisely, the concepts, opinions, and perceptions associated with monoculturalism and tolerance must be abandoned completely.

On the contrary, each of the remaining levels of the Nieto sequence of acceptance, respect, affirmation, solidarity, and critique must be endorsed and prioritized by educators as inherently fundamental to the family engagement process. Each of these reflects interpersonal and intrapersonal benefits conducive to the relationship building and relationship maintenance process. Therefore, each must be celebrated so that the integration of these robust levels create what I innovatively refer to as *engagement fusion*.

I define engagement fusion as the process of blending and saturating all the powerful components of acceptance, respect, affirmation, solidarity, and critique into all protocols related to educational providers working with parents, guardians, and the primary caregivers as a cohesive team for the benefit of student growth and development.

In as much as engagement fusion accentuates the interconnectedness among each of these levels, power and fortification emanate as the partnership between home and the school solidifies. For this reason, the triune structure of engagement fusion produces several unrivaled outcomes. Each of these will be explored in this section.

1. Engagement fusion results in the needs of each student being met inclusively without being minimized, clouded, or erased by factors of interference originating from misunderstandings resulting from miscommunications, just to name a few detrimental factors. Accordingly, emphasis is placed upon the following dimensions of the whole student during mutual interactions between the educational provider and the family:

   • Interpersonal, intrapersonal, social, emotional, intellectual, physical, spiritual, and psychomotor or kinesthetic development
   • The development of a positive self-concept
   • Addressing behavioral, mental, and physical health concerns
   • The facilitation of self-discovery, which fosters the development of talents and special abilities

   These needs are met in two significant ways. First of all, those who educate students directly utilize a tiered system ranging from a lesser to a broader, more intense level of enrichment opportunities and supportive interventions. Secondly, the family adheres to educational prescriptions provided by educators for more personal help like participating in independent practice, along with guided practice as well as receiving additional and more intensive services and instructions outside of the learning environment.

2. Engagement fusion facilitates the steady growth of students. Thus, children and young people make continuous academic and performance gains. In the end, compared to their peers who have partially or totally disengaged families or those invisible to the educational or developmental process of their children, engagement fusion produces learners who achieve at increased levels. Such students are better equipped to advance to higher levels of education and specialized training in the future. More succinctly, these learners are better positioned to welcome a future filled with great promise.

3. Engagement fusion releases harmony and peace between the family and educational system. Simply stated, both parties function as a unified, cohesive team devoted to producing exemplary developmental results for children and young people.

At no time will engagement fusion evoke any of the following adverse circumstances, emotions, or reactions between the family and school due to discord:

- Hostility
- Tension
- Anxiety
- Blame
- Conflict
- Shock
- Anger

- Frustration
- Anguish
- Distress
- Panic
- Exasperation
- Discomfort
- Hysteria
- Disillusionment
- Infuriation
- Resentment
- Struggle
- Suspicion
- Crisis
- Indignation
- Trepidation
- Agitation
- Bad feelings

Preferably, engagement fusion conceives and releases the following influential, impressive, and extraordinary benefits among the family, as well as teachers, schools, educational policy makers, and so on:

- Compatibility
- Mutuality
- Rapport
- Goodwill
- Orderliness
- Collegiality
- Undividedness

- Neighborliness
- Synergism
- Benevolence
- Communion
- Favor
- Agreement
- Fellowship
- Reconciliation
- Cooperation
- Camaraderie
- Cheerfulness
- Togetherness
- Cordiality
- Amicableness
- Homogeneousness
- Consideration
- Integrity
- Grace
- Consensus

4. Engagement fusion builds capacity for school personnel and families to combine forces to confront problems and other points of conflict with confident determination fueled with the intrinsic belief that resolution will reign supreme. The brute strength of family engagement overrides debilitated or incapacitated obstacles that could diminish collaborative efforts.

In conclusion, by synthesizing each of the acceptance, respect, affirmation, solidarity, and critique levels of family engagement, engagement fusion results. Blending these three powerful levels of family engagement with fidelity adds a highly substantial dimension of greatness to all processes related to teachers, coaches, administrators, various instructors, board of school directors, and so on, as well as families working together cohesively for the benefit of the growth and development of student.

Enthusiasm is the electricity of life. How do you get it? You act enthusiastic until you make it a habit. (Gordon Parks)

Chapter 8

Vigorous Engagement Fusion Strategies: Illustrations and Recommendations

This chapter is dedicated to providing professionals who work in or are affiliated with educational entities and facilitate, promote, and are responsible for the academic growth, creative—as well as kinesthetic, spiritual, behavioral, or mental health—and interpersonal or intrapersonal development of children and young people with concrete techniques to stimulate and maintain engagement fusion initiatives within their learning environments. Enlivened examples and suggestions follow.

1. A welcoming school environment that emanates happiness, warmth, kindness, and friendship must prevail. Specific indicators include the following examples:

    - Families receiving hearty and sincere verbal greetings by all the employees who nonverbally confirm their reception with a smile. Such greetings extend from the time the family initially enters the facility and extends through the duration of their stay.
    - Welcome posters, signs, slogans, and notes dedicated to greeting parents are posted in highly visible locations within the school and located at entrances.
    - Verbal encounters initiated by the professional staff to the family remain respectful and non-challenging.

- The sounds that parents hear while in the educational environment are pleasant to listen to and continuously accentuate positivity. This gives the parents a sense of peace.
- The physical environment is welcoming because the educational setting is clean, bright, and aesthetically pleasing.
- The inviting feeling tone of the school reflects a level of comfort synonymous to home. As a result, families experience a sense of well-being, security, and contentment in relation to their connection with the school.
- Families new to the learning environment receive welcome informational resources like a handbook, a personalized greeting card or letter, and other mementos. These families also receive an invitation to participate in welcome events like orientations, meet-and-greet gatherings, and so on.
- Beginning-of-the-year activities are organized for all families to celebrate the start of a new year or term, as well as an opportunity to learn and grow together. This includes giving families a chance to tour the school and classroom, giving time for the younger learners to become comfortable with his or her personal desk, and allowing the family and student to practice following their child's schedule and basic routines like visiting the cafeteria. Such occasions also help all families to become a valued member of the educational community.

2. Maintaining an open-door policy, which gives parents full access to educators in their work environment, is not always a feasible or reasonable expectation for various professional reasons. However, sustaining open lines of communications with

families about their availability is. Using various methods that let families know when they are available to answer questions, to listen to concerns, and to provide feedback about the growth and development of their child by sharing student work samples or performance data encompasses engagement fusion. Some of these methods designated for the abovementioned communication purposes include:

- displaying drop-in hours at workplace sites,
- distributing message cards highlighting dedicated time slots,
- utilizing social media outlets to post information, and
- adding reminders on printed materials sent to the home.

3. The creation of innovative programs specifically designed for families to facilitate their individual growth and development either on site, within the community setting, or at local or regional college or technical schools. Support mechanisms like workshops, camps, conferences, open house events, and so on should also be diligently integrated into these efforts.

4. A strategically identified faculty member, center worker, or district-wide employee who is genuinely passionate about and values the establishment of families as partners and knowledgeable about research-based strategies, as well as best practices connected to this area, should be given the responsibility to advance localized engagement efforts. Developing an organizational vision and mission statement, along with beliefs and values associated with family engagement, should begin the course of action. This leader should possess the capacity to organize, empower, and inspire others within the organization to enthusiastically

embrace initiatives that he or she either creates or endorses that are aligned to his or her unique educational or programming goals. The professional should also assume the responsibility of continuously evaluating universal engagement efforts.

5. Developing and enforcing systemic, building-wide, classroom-family, or program-specific engagement policies.

6. Annual commemorative and celebratory traditions should be established. This may include culturally based observances as well. Such school-based rituals will empower families to use their voice to collaborate with educators and assume leadership roles as they function as a team to plan together, offer suggestions, give their feedback, share their authentic experiences, donate distinctive resources, and provide the much-needed assistance during unique occasions.

7. Despite the fact that levels of confidentiality must be honored within educational settings, there are times when teachers and instructors, administrators, coaches, and others who facilitate student development must maintain an honest degree of communications with the families they serve. This is known as transparency. When educators are open about concerns and incidents, again, that will not compromise private information, unquestionable trust results. The family, then, has complete faith in the professional as well as the program that their child participates in.

8. Educators should activate love, support, encouragement, and concern when the family experiences tough times in an unconditional manner that reflects sincerity and humility. These emotional responses should manifest in countless ways and depend upon the individualized needs of the family, along with the depth of anguish and despair that they experience.

Straightforwardly stated, these professionals should extend a helping hand and comfort to families in crisis.

9. The communications between the home and the educational facility should be consistent. Varied formats should be utilized to share information. Examples include:

- Personal letters, notes, and postcards mailed home, as well as placed in communication folders and student mailboxes, which are hand carried home
- Automated telephone messages
- Using technologies like social media and Web pages to post periodic memoranda
- Frequent newsletters
- Developing and revising on-site message boards
- Maintaining family resource centers at the educational center
- Periodic informational meetings held at the learning facilities and at central locations within the communities where students reside
- Making "good news" telephone calls or sending email messages home along with those to share concerns
- Displaying information on bulletin boards within the community at specified locations such as the library, grocery store, or place of worship
- Facilitating various meetings by way of video conference at the school, the home of the student, or a mutually agreed upon location
- Having brief discussions during informal encounters

A critical component of the communication process includes providing parents with advance notice of events and activities, such as letting them know the dates and times of family-oriented meetings and dispatching immediate communications in the form of a parent letter or various technologies if the health, safety, and well-being of the learners have been compromised in any way. Educators should endeavor to publish and distribute a calendar of events to families at the start of a school year or educational sequence.

10. Developing and implementing a uniform home-visiting procedure completed by a pair of educators to facilitate the process of meeting with parents in their area of comfort. While the family home would be the ideal location to meet, the home visit may take place at a community coffee shop or restaurant, during an enjoyable walk in the community, or while the parent is on a break at work. The initial purpose of these meetings is to formulate relationships with the families by getting to know them by engaging in a meaningful conversation with them. This is primarily accomplished by giving parents a chance to discuss their hopes and dreams for their children and to discuss information about their cultural background. The secondary purpose of the home visit is for follow-up purposes, such as to share specific data about the progress of learners, to offer suggestions for support, and to work to stabilize the relationship between the family and the educational provider if a strong partnership has not been concretely established.

11. Families should be given opportunities to share in some of the appropriate decision-making processes in some managerial

phases of the instructional program. Empowerment, ownership, and pride result.

12. Parental input committees and advisory teams should be established to provide families with a forum to exchange ideas about the educational program that their child participates in. These meeting sessions should be facilitated by program, school, and district-wide leaders and policy makers. This collaborative process will enable opinions to be exchanged so that decisions will be made for the betterment of student development and the instructional program. The result of this practice is that the voice of the family is valued.

13. Providing chances for families to utilize their unique talents and gifts, specialized skills, and designated experiences by making significant contributions through service within the learning environment creates powerful opportunities for them to become meaningfully engaged. Additionally, highly organized volunteer programs have the capacity to enrich and supplement the support provided to learners and the delivery of quality instruction. Families are validated with educators rely upon their assistance.

14. Hosting appreciation events for all parents to express gratitude for whatever level of support that they provide. This appreciation effort will encourage as well as motivate families to become more determined to be engaged at deeper, more impactful levels.

15. Conferences should be highly structured and organized so that parents are provided with the information that will be discussed ahead of time. As one exclusive example, families should receive performance data about the child prior to the traditional parent-teacher conference. This will enable the family to carefully analyze the information to be reviewed so that they will have

an adequate amount of time to formulate questions that will be presented to the teacher. In essence, the family will be able to prepare for the discussion. The educational provider should ensure that the amount of time scheduled for the conference will be sufficient to ensure that family concerns are addressed. Providing this type of supportive accommodation results in parental satisfaction.

16. Encouraging advocacy efforts through organizations such as the PTA (Parent-Teacher Association) or PTO (Parent-Teacher Organization). Such organized efforts empower families by activating their voice.

17. Suggesting that parents work with designated community service providers and agencies that have the capacity to help support the unique needs of their children or family unit. Some of these service providers that give them the chance to connect with external community collaborators may include these professionals:

- Private instructors, tutors, and coaches
- Neighborhood partners from the faith-based community
- Behavioral, mental, and physical health providers such as counselors, therapists, psychiatrists, neurologists, social workers, a therapeutic support staff member, and psychologists

18. Professional flexibility must prevail as accommodations that provide designated provisions for families as they engage with the schools are made. Some of these comprise:

- Providing language interpreters for families who are English learners as they participate in on-site events, along with interpreting written communications sent to the home; this also includes securing sign language interpreters as required
- Remaining mindful of parental work schedules as events such as various conferences and meetings are planned
- Modifying printed materials distributed to parents like copying the documents using larger print
- Ensuring that specified family dietary needs are addressed when food is served at the educational facility during specified occasions
- Making sure that individualized accommodations are made for any family who needs assistance such as special seating, ramps, and operational elevators, as well as other facility supports that conform to ADA (Americans with Disabilities Act) Standards for Accessible Design

The abovementioned illustrations represent a tremendously extensive list of the promising ways that educators are able to incorporate engagement fusion techniques into their management processes relevant to collaborative opportunities with families. However, when educational providers release their imaginative powers translated into vibrant creativity, many more engagement fusion possibilities are cultivated.

You cannot discover new oceans unless you have the courage to lose sight of the shore. (Unknown)

Chapter 9

Engagement Fusion Propels and Mobilizes Social Justice

As previously examined in the last two chapters, engagement fusion powerfully solidifies the capacity of families to establish and sustain profound interactions and relationships with various educational providers by infusing all the dynamic characteristics of acceptance, respect, and affirmation, solidarity, and critique while the notion of monoculturalism and tolerance are utterly abandoned. Additionally, all of the creative engagement fusion exemplars and ideas that may be successfully adopted into educational and developmental best practices substantiates the intensity of this strategy designed for families to be partners throughout all educational progressions involving their children.

The final compelling and undeniable advantage of engagement fusion relevant to the realm of education is robustly connected to social justice. In the context of family engagement, social justice refers to a democratic process in which parents and guardians are freely given the autonomy and the privilege to share as well as balance their power with the power of educational providers for the benefit of the learning experience of their children. As those responsible for the delivery of any type of educational services to students adhere to an unblemished ethical as well as principled code of professional conduct, social justice preserves the civil rights of families to become active and honored participants in the learning process because they are given equitable opportunities to:

- use their voice to contribute to many decision-making processes that permeate the educational environment;
- build their capacity to develop their individualized strengths and unique abilities to support initiatives designated to improve identified segments within the educational realm and to celebrate professional efforts for their child;
- share factual and authentic data about sectors within the learning environment that require attention, revisions, and supports to policy makers in an effort to effect positive change; and
- exercise their right and freedom to expect mutual as well as open lines of communications pertaining to their child, including information that compromises their health, safety, and well-being, along with broad streams of information relative to educational programming.

In addition to these unchallengeable rights, two significant outcomes become apparent. These unquestionable effects follow:

1. *Apathy is abolished.* The social justice aspect of engagement fusion empowers and inspires the family to willfully contribute to the educational process of their children in a consistent and substantial manner. Because of this, the notion of parental apathy is severed at the root of its existence. Family disengagement elements associated with indifference, insensitivity, and disinterest are foreign to the engagement process. Parental unresponsiveness, detachment, and aloofness are nonexistent because the relationship between the family and school is energized by the liberties deeply embedded within the foundational values associated with social justice. Therefore,

families are consistently welcomed as active and equal partners as a result of this paradigm.

> The greatest danger to our future is apathy. (Jane Goodall)

> Apathy is the acceptance of the unacceptable. (John Scott)

2. *Fear is eradicated.* Fear refers to the sense of uneasiness, suspicion, or anxiety experienced by an educator who has reservations or misgivings about the constitutional freedom extended to families to establish a cohesive interpersonal bond with them. Social justice results in the bold identification of specific fears aligned with interpersonal contact and exchanges, especially among those classified as multicultural. These foreboding emotions, along with other powerfully offensive feelings profoundly connected to hatred, such as detestation and disgust, include but are not limited to the following:

- Alethephobia—the fear of truth and transparency
- Allodoxaphobia—the fear of the opinions of others
- Anthropophobic—the fear of people within a specific society
- Athazagoraphobic—the fear of being ignored or replaced
- Biphobia—the hatred of bisexual individuals
- Cenophobia—the fear of new ideas or situations
- Dikephobia—the fear of justice
- Eleatherophobia—the fear of freedom
- Epistemophobia—the fear of knowledge
- Ethnophobia—the fear or hatred of any racial group or ethnicity except one's own

- Gerontophobia—the hatred of the elderly
- Haptephobia—the fear of being touched
- Homophobic—the strong dislike or hatred of homosexual individuals
- Ideophobic—the fear of ideas
- Kainolophobic—the fear of anything new
- Ligyrophobia—the fear of loud voices
- Methathesiophobia—the fear of change
- Monophobia—the fear of being in close proximity to others
- Peniaphobia—the fear of poverty and poor people
- Philophobia—the fear of love and compassion
- Prosophobia—the fear of progress
- Psychophobia—the fear or hatred of people with any mental or behavioral health diagnosis
- Social phobia—the fear of social interactions with other people
- Soteriophobia—the fear of being dependent on another person
- Theophobia—the fear of religious ideas other than one's own
- Transphobia—the fear or hatred of transsexual individuals
- Xenoglossophobia—the fear of foreign languages
- Xenophobia—the fear or hatred of individuals from foreign countries

Social justice unequivocally destroys anxieties, dread, and doubt regarding the establishment of empowered family partnerships because the all practices embedded within the engagement fusion protocol releases a collegial spirit of peace, unity, and reconciliation. All these, including many other social apprehensions and worries, are purged through engagement fusion. To paraphrase the latter idea, engagement fusion overrides fear.

I have learned that courage was not the absence of fear, but the triumph over it. The brave man is not he who does not feel afraid, but he who conquers that fear. (Nelson Mandela)

3. *A democracy prevails.* The intentionally known motto that has been historically embedded into the fabric of the society of the United States, "*E pluribus unum*," has been interpreted as "out of many, one." This credo is synonymous to the democratic process because it symbolizes the significance of one individual within a community, village, or society of countless citizens and counterparts. This idea can be further examined to stand for the power that one singular voice has to impact social processes connected to justice, decision-making, empowerment, equity, freedom, and equality.

In the context of social justice, engagement fusion preserves, embodies, and honors the democracy of all families. Engagement protocols that reflect this enable collaborative efforts among the families, teachers, administrators, or other professionals who functions as an educator or a developer of children and young people to serve with dignity. This means that the family will be held in high esteem by educators as they work for the ultimate good for the overall developmental experience for their children.

I understand democracy as something that gives the weak the same chances of the strong. (Mahatma Gandhi)

In summary, engagement fusion mobilizes social justice. All the aforementioned elements of social justice, along with those associated with the privilege of the family to be given the opportunity to be empowered to function as an equal partner in the education of their children, becomes activated. As stated earlier, because apathy and fear are nonexistent and the democratic process abounds as the family works in a collegial manner with the school, the supreme outcome is that all educators and all parents form a professional coalition and are joined together through engagement fusion. Both parties rally in unison to advance social justice for the inclusive developmental benefit of children and young people.

> Every great dream begins with a dreamer. Always remember, you have within you the strength, the patience, and the passion to reach for the stars to change the world. (Harriett Tubman)

Chapter 10

What Engagement Fusion Does Not Encompass

As it has been thoroughly presented in previous chapters, the successful integration of engagement fusion into any formalized structure dedicated to developing, educating, nurturing, supporting, and treating children and young people has the capacity to substantially increase the numbers of families who formulate and sustain meaningful partnerships with them. This is especially true for the families who have historically been underrepresented as active participants in such processes that impact their children. Despite the numerous benefits that result from the seamless implementation of authentic engagement fusion, it is important to examine the conditions which exist that prevent this type of partnership from being released. This final chapter is devoted to the factors that do not encompass engagement fusion. Each of these circumstances follows:

Family Interference

Anytime leaders within an organization habitually distribute authority and control to families, which overrides the authority and control of the professionals within the learning environment, engagement fusion efforts become obstructed. While the professional providers who work to service the needs of students join the families of their pupils in desiring each learner to achieve at his or her highest level, it becomes problematic when organizational leaders do not delineate the boundaries that separate these employees from the parents. This division exists because the educator has either gained expertise or is refining their level of expertise as experience and professional development are acquired and because it is the family who possesses a deep knowledge of the multifaceted dimensions of their child. Conflict and confusion erupt when the family fails to understand that being an active partner does not include disregarding the abovementioned boundaries by attempting to assume the role of the educator or by endeavoring to provide the educator with recommendations for performing their role according to their individualized specifications. Simply stated, this results in parental interference in the educational process.

It is the responsibility of leaders within a school, school district, or developmental program such as the principal, superintendent, or program director to clearly define the standards of engagement fusion. This must be accomplished in two ways.

First of all, the leaders must clearly articulate the expectations so that families honor the professional expertise boundaries within their learning environment. These expectancies may be communicated to parents using various formats that include but are not limited to verbalizing them during small and large group parent meetings, conferences, and gatherings and developing, displaying, and distributing various communication-utilizing forums, such as newsletters, social media, and personal letters.

Secondly, the leaders must model engagement fusion protocols. Demonstrating such procedures and behaviors that encompass all the unique elements of acceptance, respect, affirmation, solidarity, and critique will establish the standards and expectations that families are able to faultlessly follow as well as adhere to.

Family Distrust

Some families are unable to develop the mutual relationship required for the manifestation of the elements of engagement fusion with the educational providers because of the lack of trust. Such parents either deeply question or have lost complete confidence in the educational provider having the capacity to service the unique developmental of neither needs and goals of their child nor the ability of these professionals to relate to them as mutual partners who are capable of making contributions to the collaborative process.

There are reasons for this lack of faith in the educational institution as well as the instructional process. These explanations are elaborated below.

The past educational experiences of the family have the capacity to influence the current interpersonal responses that they assume in relation to the school. Whether in the same school or district or in a totally different instructional facility, or whether with the same instructional provider or with another one, such derogatory occurrences may have taken place while the parent was enrolled in school or during the time that their child was a student. Despite the specific period of time, the precise location, or the impacted member of the family, suppressed memories of the adverse incidents awaken all the intense emotions of anger, humiliation, embarrassment, sadness, agitation, and so on that are connected to the past. Engagement fusion cannot be planted in the soil filled with the unresolved conflicts of the past.

When a family observes or when their child becomes the victim of blatant or subtle injustices within the organization, trust will not exist. Targeted unfairness, inequalities, prejudice, bigotry, discrimination, bias, hatred, disrespect, and stereotyping results in the family losing confidence in the integrity of the program. As previously analyzed in the section of the book relevant to social justice, engagement fusion will not grow if it is chocked by the weeds of social offenses.

In order to help the family with legitimate trust issues who are filled with despair overcome this problematic state, educators must exercise patience. Calculated, incremental small steps must be taken to establish trust between the family and the school. Each interpersonal parental encounter initiated by the professional, along with nonverbal nuances communicated to them, should be reassuring. Genuine kindness, friendliness, and compassion must also prevail during these interactions. These efforts will ultimately enable the family to develop confidence in the educational provider so that trust will cultivate and grow. In doing so, engagement fusion will flourish.

The Overwhelmed Family

Challenging economic circumstances, social conditions within the community in which one resides like unemployment, environmental factors, homelessness, and violence, personal problems embedded in grief, and the overall structure of some family units may result in parents being overcome with an extremely high level of anxiety, trauma, and pressure. When parents exist in a survival mode in which they are forced to work multiple jobs, when struggling to locate affordable yet safe and reliable childcare becomes a vital necessity, and when they are forced to make monetary decisions and sacrifices to meet their obligations with bills as well as groceries, school-related information, unique activities, and specialized events become secondary or even tertiary at best. Because of this, engagement fusion becomes subdued.

Despite these opposing influences, school and program personnel have the ability to grow engagement fusion. The initial process includes adopting a nonjudgmental disposition by empathizing with the life situations encountered by the families being served. Next, regardless of the depth of family engagement, all the efforts that are made should always be acknowledged by the educator extrinsically. The face-to-face or personal recognition of occasional small family engagement efforts, like expressing gratitude to the parent when the child attends school and is dressed nicely, having a school document signed, and the child reporting to school with homework signed or a skill practiced provide the parent with encouragement. Regardless of the stress experienced by the family, such encouragement will open the door to deeper levels of engagement. Additionally, educators who work to support struggling families by connecting them to resource providers who will deliver various types of assistance and by extending an act of kindness, such as lending a listening ear when the family simply needs someone to talk to during difficult times, stimulates the progression of engagement fusion.

Family Apathy

Despite the fact that engagement fusion produces powerful outcomes for students and their families, and even though schools implement this participatory approach, there may be some families who willfully maintain a spirit of indifference to the process. The lack of concern for this protocol, the apathy displayed relevant to improving the educational condition of their children, and the unresponsiveness to the efforts of the educational providers to embrace as well as to reciprocate the indicators of this type of engagement will prevent families from connecting with educational providers interpersonally. These disinterested parents will never be positioned as equal partners with their child's school because they lack the intrinsic motivation and the instinctive desire to care.

Educators must remain genuinely committed to completely eradicating family apathy. The professionals must employ dynamic communication techniques, which includes other engagement fusion strategies outlined earlier in this text. Additionally, teachers, coaches, principals, and others who educate children and young people must share authentic examples of the success of these learners when families are partners as engagement fusion develops.

The Egotistical Family

Educators may encounter families who feign a passion for the entire process of education. These parents may deceive the leadership and other staff members within their child's developmental or academic program to believe that they possess enthusiasm for all the collaborative initiatives exemplified, including but not limited to a chance to have their voice heard so that some of the decision-making is shared, along with sustained extremely positive relationships with the professionals within the organization. Unfortunately, as the professional interactions with such families deepen, their actual motives for being so actively engaged become apparent. The reality is that the involvement of these parents is solely due to narcissistic, self-absorbed tendencies that emerge from their quest for power, control, and notoriety within the organization. Genuine acceptance, respect, affirmation, solidarity, and critique vital for engagement fusion are prohibited from being revealed as well as developing.

School and program leaders must be among the first educators to confront such families by having courageous and honest conversations with them so that the attention is strategically removed from them and refocused on the needs of their child. More challenging cases may require the assistance of a neutral mediator who will work with the school in an effort to resolve the relational problems that erupt due to the egotistical family.

Family Negativity

Any family who fails to maintain a positive disposition, healthy outlook, or confident attitude during interactions with professionals within the learning environment prohibits the manifestation of engagement fusion. Some of the examples of destructive parental traits detrimental to engagement efforts include those shown below:

- Demeaning verbal and nonverbal actions that result in the professional being made to feel incompetent, devalued, and disrespected
- Displaying harassing and bullying behaviors that are aimed at employees
- Undermining the authority of school district, school, and program leadership, as well as those responsible for educating youth
- Demanding and otherwise expecting preferential treatment
- Assuming a harsh, confrontational, defensive, and argumentative temperament
- Disrupting the peace, harmony, and balance within the educational atmosphere
- Attempting to compromise ethical principles for personal gain
- Refusing to validate the perspective, opinion, and experience of the educator
- Resisting the collaborative engagement efforts that the school extends

As with family apathy, the engagement fusion suggestions provided in this book should be used as references for facilitating the transformation of negative families into those filled with optimism. The power of positivity must also be exemplified as all school personnel models appropriate attitudes and behaviors.

Most significantly, educational leaders as well as others who are adversely impacted, must have a private and robust face-to-face conversation with the negative family to reiterate the interpersonal standards that the school maintains and to advise them that their unacceptable attitudes and behaviors must cease. These educators must immediately model forgiveness by not holding grudge or displaying any form of retaliation and they must work to build a relationship with the family to allow engagement fusion to begin to develop and flourish.

The Contentious Family

Critical parents are those who continuously find fault with the educational program that their child is enrolled in. Constant complaints about the professionals who deliver instruction along with other services, students enrolled in the school, the physical learning environment, among many other grievances, results in endless controversy surrounding this family. The antagonistic and touchy disposition of this type of parent destroys any hope that engagement fusion will ever develop due to several unacceptable tendencies that they display. These interpersonal faults include some of the following:

- Using various forums to breed their disapproval, such as gossiping and spreading rumors to other families as well as some of the employees within the educational facility and utilizing social media and other forms of communications to spread discord and chaos
- Disrespecting leadership and others who provide services to learners by publicly demeaning them during overt or subtle interactions
- Dishonoring protocols relevant to confidentiality by secretly nudging some individuals that they trust within the organization for private information and their knowledge in a smug manner
- Monopolizing the time of educators while they are fulfilling their professional responsibilities within the workplace as well as when they are off-duty for nonemergency purposes without regard for their occupational and personal obligations

All the advice for responding to the negative family must be adhered to in a seamless manner so that the school which promotes engagement fusion is able to do so. In addition to all of these proposals, more intensive strategies must be employed to correct the appalling conduct of the contentious family. These sanctions include the following.

- School, district, or program leadership is urged to develop a formal written communication to this family that an official meeting will need to be held to discuss their demeaning, crude, despicable conduct
- Once the meeting is held, the family should be informed of all the concerns that they have, including the harmful effect their behaviors have on the educational program
- An opportunity must be given for the family to respond
- The family must be advised that their derogatory behaviors must cease and desist; the leader may offer support to the family in doing so such as conflict resolution
- If the families agree to stop, the educational leadership must immediately assume the aforementioned posture of forgiveness as they build a relationship with them to facilitate the ultimate development of engagement fusion
- Conversely, further actions will be required for the contentious family who refuses to take adopt a more appropriate disposition
- Depending on the type of educational facility that serves the learner, such as a private school or extracurricular program, the family may need to be asked to withdraw
- In the event that a public school is involved, some of the following options may be employed: the family may be transferred to another school within the same district or another education program such as an online school to provide them with a fresh

start in a new environment; the parents may be prohibited from entering the school or having direct contact with school personnel for a probationary period of time; disorderly conduct citations may be issued for future incidents; legal support may be obtained, such as the development of a Memorandum of Understanding that will ensure the school that the behaviors exhibited by the family will be appropriate

Because of the severity of such aforementioned cases involving the contentious family, engagement fusion is not an option within the impacted learning environments.

Despite some of the adversity and resistance factors associated with the full integration of engagement fusion into any academic and developmental environs, as well as any other professional, extracurricular, human services, or faith-based setting devoted to supporting children and youth, patience and perseverance are critical. By modeling steadfast persistence, endurance, and determination in a tireless manner, educational providers will ultimately reap the positive benefits associated with the establishment of parental partnerships reflective of engagement fusion.

> You may encounter many defeats, but you must not be
> defeated. In fact, it may be necessary to encounter the defeats
> so you know who you are, what you can rise from, how you
> still come out of it. (Maya Angelou)

References

BrainyQuote. 2016 and 2017. n.d. Retrieved from https://plus.google.com/brainyquotes.

Every Student Succeeds Act, Public Law 114–95. 2015. (114th Congress S. 1177).

Leonard, Agatha. 2016. Assistant to the Superintendent, Special Education and Pupil Personnel Services, Pittsburgh, PA,

Nieto, Sonia. 2004. *Affirming Diversity: The Sociopolitical Context of Multicultural Education, Fourth Edition*. Edited by Stephen D. Dragin. Boston, MA: Allyn and Bacon, Pearson Education Inc.

Nieto, Sonia, "Profoundly Multicultural Questions", Educational Leadership. December 2002- January 2003, page 6-10, V 60, n 4.

No Child Left Behind Act of 2001. Public Law 107–110. 2002. Volume 20. United States Code.

Vereen, Deborah M. 2006. "Affirmation Descriptors."

Wikipedia. 2017. "Self-Fulfilling Prophecy." Retrieved from https://en.m.wikipedia.org.

Index

About the Author

Dr. Deborah M. Vereen has held various professional positions in the field of education for more than thirty-five years. Her earliest experience includes serving as family and consumer sciences teacher in the Pittsburgh Public Schools, the Belle Vernon Area School District, and the North Allegheny School District for a total of thirteen years. Deborah credits her instructional content area for providing her with a solid foundation for establishing and maintaining substantive relationships with the parents of the students that she served. Her value of positive parental partnerships continued as her level of educational responsibility increased.

Deborah served as Assistant Principal and Principal within the aforementioned North Allegheny School District and the Woodland Hills School District for a total of twenty two years. She also served as adjunct professor of multicultural education at the graduate level during this time for a combined total of thirteen years at Seton Hill University and Chatham University. As Deborah developed the curriculum for her courses, she also began to develop a deep appreciation for the research of Dr. Sonia Nieto as it relates to "the Levels of Multicultural Education." Without ever meeting Dr. Nieto, Deborah began actively applying the research of Dr. Nieto to her professional interactions with her professional colleagues, college students, and the parents of the students enrolled in her schools. In doing so, she personalized and extended the work of Dr. Nieto by developing the Affirmation Descriptors in an effort to help other educators reach the highest multicultural level that included affirmation, solidarity, and critique.

Another professional experience that Deborah participated in within the Woodland Hills School District includes serving as the Director of Pupil Personnel Services for one year. She also fulfilled her professional mission as well as her individual passion of promoting dynamic stages of family engagement by formerly serving as the Assistant to the Superintendent of Family and Community Engagement and Volunteerism.

Deborah received her formalized basic education within the Pittsburgh public schools. Her undergraduate degree was obtained at West Virginia Wesleyan College while her graduate and doctoral degrees were earned at Duquesne University. In addition to the abovementioned family and consumer sciences, her other areas of collegiate study include elementary and secondary school administration and educational leadership.

While the completion of this book represents a two-year journey for Deborah, she celebrates the forum that she has been blessed to have to share her dynamic message of engagement fusion. In doing so, she believes that children and young people will achieve, grow, and perform at optimum, record-breaking levels as they conquer challenges, embrace their potential, develop interpersonally, and mature as learners. The advantages of engagement fusion will extend into adulthood and beyond.

Deborah is an extremely proud mother of a precious daughter enrolled in middle school who is the constant source of her motivation and inspiration.

CPSIA information can be obtained
at www.ICGtesting.com
Printed in the USA
BVHW080238110119
537596BV00001B/105/P

9 781543 445442